Visit BibleHelps.info

Contents

Note: All Scripture quotations I've included are from the NIV, but feel free to use any translation you prefer.

Jesus' Miracles

The miracles of Jesus show us both who and what His passion is. He is the God who can order nature and the God who loves us enough to do so for our benefit. He's the God who requires our faith and the one who rewards us by giving us a taste of His kingdom.

The lessons I've included in this volume cover a sampling of Christ's mighty acts from after the Sermon on the Mount until Holy Week.

Each of the 16 lessons in this volume has games, crafts, and other activities to help you teach the stories and to help the kids apply the message. I'm also including a list of resources you might want to add to the lessons to make them that much better.

Recommended Extras

You don't need anything extra to use the lessons. I will, however, provide some suggestions you might find helpful. You can use these resources in addition to or instead of the ideas I've provided.

Here are the resources I recommend for the entire series. I'll list story-specific resources at the end of each lesson.

The Complete Illustrated Children's Bible — for telling the stories with beautiful artwork and Biblical accuracy

The Beginner's Bible: Timeless Stories for Children — for telling the stories to younger children

Superbook: The Miracles of Jesus and Jesus Heals the Blind – animated videos from the updated Superbook series, includes time-traveling children who learn lessons from the story

The Greatest Adventure Stories from the Bible: The Miracles of Jesus – animated video with time-traveling teenagers who witness the Biblical story, realistic art style

Greatest Heroes and Legends of the Bible: Miracles of Jesus – another animated video with a Disneyesque art style and no time traveling

Manga Comic Book: Messiah – for your classroom or church library

My Big Book of Bible Heroes Devotional – a devotional to recommend for families or older students

Jesus Wants to Help Us!

Use this children's Sunday School lesson to help kids think of how Jesus can help them and how they can thank Him.

Needed: Bibles, various objects, a picture of someone with leprosy, a ball, drawing paper, crayons or colored pencils

> https://commons.wikimedia.org/wiki/File:An_introducti on_to_dermatology_(1905)_nodular_leprosy.jpg

Intro Game: No! – Have the students line up single file behind a line in your play area. Between them and you is an area where they will play tag. You will stand or sit at the other side of the play area with a variety of objects in front of you. One of the objects could be a sample of a snack you're going to give the kids at the end of the game. Choose one of the objects to be the key object for each round. One leader or volunteer student will be "It" in the middle of the play area.

The first student will run up to you and ask you for one of the objects in front of you. If it's the key object you chose, they win the game. If it isn't, say "No!" That student then remains in the center play area. They then have to run from It. If they get tagged, they go to the back of the line.

The next student runs up to you as soon as the previous one receives their answer.

Let the snack be the last correct answer. When a student asks for it, end the game and pass out the snacks.

As the students are eating, start the lesson.

Lesson: (Note: Always allow students enough time to think about and to give their answers to the questions before clarifying the teaching.)

(Read Matthew 8:1-2.)

"When Jesus came down from the mountainside, large crowds followed Him. A man with leprosy came and knelt before Him and said, 'Lord, if You are willing, You can make me clean.'"

The man in this story had leprosy. What is leprosy?

(Show picture of someone with leprosy.) Leprosy is a disease that affects your skin. It can get so bad that your skin rots, and it can make your nose or your fingers or other body parts start falling off.

People made the man in this story him live outside of town, and they wouldn't touch him because of his disease.

But the man came up to Jesus and said, "Lord, if You are willing, You can make me clean." He said Jesus could make him better.

Do you think Jesus will help the man get better?

Would you touch someone who had leprosy and looked like that?

(Read Matthew 8:3.)

"Jesus reached out His hand and touched the man. 'I am willing,' He said. 'Be clean!' Immediately he was cleansed of his leprosy."

Jesus did touch the man who looked like that. He touched the man and said, "I am willing to help you."

And the man was all better!

Jesus touched him because the thing about Jesus is that He doesn't care what people look like or if they're scary or gross or if they smell bad. Jesus just wants to help people. And if you ask Him, He will help you too. He might not always help you in the same way that He helped the man with leprosy, but He will help you somehow.

Jesus said He was willing to help the man. Jesus will never say "no" when You ask Him for help. He might not help you in the way that you want Him to help you, but He will always help you somehow.

What do you think are some ways that Jesus can help you?

If you're sad, Jesus can give you hope. If you're scared, He can make you brave. If you need help to be better, He can give you strength. If you're sick, He can heal you.

How can you ask Jesus to help you? (Pray.)

And why do You think Jesus wants to help people so much? (Jesus loves people.)

Prayer Activity: Asking Jesus for Help – Have students spread out around the room and pray silently. Direct them to tell Jesus about something they want help with. Then, after a minute, have them ask Jesus for His help. Finally, have them listen silently for Jesus to say anything in their heart.

Lesson Continues: Read Matthew 8:4.

"Then Jesus said to him, 'See that you don't tell anyone. But go, show yourself to the priest and offer the gift Moses commanded, as a testimony to them.'"

Jesus told the man to go to the Temple and to give a gift to the church. Why do you think Jesus told him to do that?

5

When God or Jesus does something for us, we should show our thankfulness to Him. One way people can do that is by giving a special gift to God out of their money.

That's a good way to tell God thanks for helping you. There are also other ways of thanking God. What are some other ways of thanking God that you can think of? (Saying thank you in a prayer, doing something nice for someone else, trying to do what God wants you to do more, etc.)

Game: Thanks Toss – Students stand in a circle and randomly toss a ball back and forth. Whenever someone catches the ball, they have to name one thing they're thankful for, but it can't be anything anyone else has said.

Craft: Thanking Jesus – Give students drawing supplies and have them draw one way that they can thank Jesus for helping them. When everyone is finished, have them explain their drawings.

Closing Prayer: Jesus, thank You that You are always willing to help us. And when we do ask You for help, help us to remember that You will help us in Your way, not always in the way we want You to help us. Amen.

Recommended Extra

Jesus Heals a Leper – free coloring and activity pages

> https://freesundayschoolcurriculum.weebly.com/uploads/1/2/5/0/12503916/lesson_32_jesus_heals_a_leper.pdf

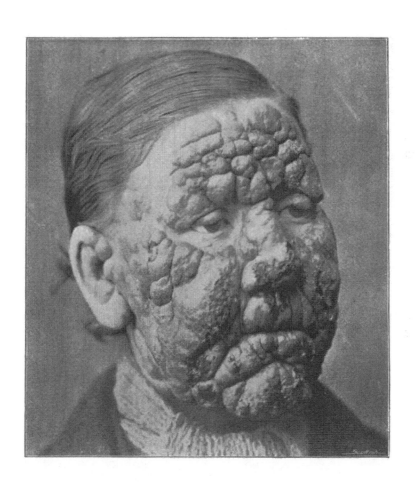

Jesus Helps Us from Far Away!

Use this children's Sunday School lesson to show kids that they can pray to Jesus even though He's not physically near.

Needed: Bibles, Faith vs. Doubt cards, telephone, drawing paper, crayons or colored pencils, "Faith" slips of paper

Intro Game: Faith vs. Doubt – Print out or write the words Doubt or Faith on a set of index cards. You should have an equal number of cards that say Faith as Doubt.

Divide students into two teams, and have the teams line up on separate sides of the room in single file lines. Mix up the cards and give each student a card that says Faith or Doubt. Set a timer for 3-5 minutes, depending on how many students you have. When you say "Go!" the first two students run toward each and show each other their cards.

If one says Faith and the other says Doubt, the student with Faith scores a point for their team. The person with Doubt does not score. If both say Faith, both score a point and if both say Doubt, neither does. Both return to the back of their lines and trade their cards for a new card.

As soon as they leave the center, the second two players run up and do the same thing. Play continues until the timer runs out. The team with the most points at the end wins.

Lesson: Read Matthew 8:5-6.

"When Jesus had entered Capernaum, a centurion came to Him, asking for help. 'Lord,' he said, 'my servant lies at home paralyzed, suffering terribly.'"

What was the problem in this story? (The man's servant was sick.)

And the man who came to ask Jesus for help was a centurion, a soldier in the Roman army who was in charge of 100 soldiers.

So, this Roman soldier comes to ask Jesus for help.

That's interesting because most Romans didn't believe in the real God, but this one must have because He came to ask Jesus for help.

(Read Matthew 8:7-13.)

"Jesus said to him, 'Shall I come and heal him?'

"The centurion replied, 'Lord, I do not deserve to have You come under my roof. But just say the word, and my servant will be healed. For I myself am a man under authority, with soldiers under me. I tell this one, "Go," and he goes; and that one, "Come," and he comes. I say to my servant, "Do this," and he does it.'

'When Jesus heard this, He was amazed and said to those following Him, 'Truly I tell you, I have not found anyone in Israel with such great faith. I say to you that many will come from the east and the west, and will take their places at the feast with Abraham, Isaac and Jacob in the kingdom of heaven. But the subjects of the kingdom will be thrown outside, into the darkness, where there will be weeping and gnashing of teeth.'

"Then Jesus said to the centurion, 'Go! Let it be done just as you believed it would.' And his servant was healed at that moment."

Jesus said He would go with the man to heal his servant, but did Jesus have to go see the servant to heal him? (No.)

The soldier told Jesus He didn't have to come with him because he had faith that Jesus can help people from far away. So, Jesus stayed right where He was and healed the servant who was probably miles away.

That's kind of like us. Jesus is far away right now, up in Heaven, but we know we can still ask Him to help us.

(Show students your phone.) Have any of you ever called someone on the telephone? When you call someone, you can talk to them even if they're really far away. And when we pray, we can talk to Jesus even though He's really far away.

We know that Jesus can help us from where He is, far away in Heaven, because He still sees us and hears us and can help us from there because He's so powerful. We simply need to have faith like the centurion did.

The centurion had so much faith that Jesus said not even the people in Israel had as much faith as him.

Even though the people of Israel were supposed to believe in God, this Roman soldier had more faith than they did. And Jesus said that anyone who had faith would get to go to Heaven, but anyone who doesn't have faith in God can't go to Heaven.

Game: Finding Faith – Before class, hide strips of paper around the room with the word "Faith" written on them. Then, divide students into two or more teams. When you say, "Go!" the team members search the room to find the slips of paper. Once someone finds a slip of paper, they return to their team's starting area and wait for the others to find theirs. The first team to have all their members find a slip of paper and make it to their team's starting area wins.

When the game is finished, remind students that we all need to have faith, and we all need to have our own faith, if we want to go to Heaven.

Craft: Long Distance Prayers – Give students drawing supplies and have them draw a picture of them praying to Jesus asking Him to help them with something. Remind them that even though Jesus is far away in Heaven, He still hears our prayers and can still help us from where He is.

Closing Prayer: Jesus, we thank You that even though You're up in Heaven, You can still hear us and help us. Help us all to have faith in You like the centurion did. Amen.

Recommended Extra

The Faith of the Centurion – free coloring and activity pages

> https://freesundayschoolcurriculum.weebly.com/uploads/1/2/5/0/12503916/lesson_34_the_faith_of_the_centurion.pdf

Jesus Calms the Storm

Use this children's Sunday School lesson to teach kids that we can always have faith and never need to be afraid.

Needed: Faith vs. Fear cards, masking tape or other supplies to make the outline of a large ship, crumpled pieces of paper

Intro Game: Faith vs. Fear – Print out or write the words Fear or Faith on a set of index cards. You should have an equal number of cards that say Faith as Fear.

Divide students into two teams, and have the teams line up on separate sides of the room in single file lines. Mix up the cards and give each student a card that says Faith or Fear. Set a timer for 3-5 minutes, depending on how many students you have. When you say Go! the first two students run toward each and show each other their cards.

If one says Faith and the other says Fear, the student with Faith scores a point for their team. The person with Fear does not score. If both say Faith, both score a point and if both say Fear, neither does. Both return to the back of their lines and trade their cards for a new card.

As soon as they leave the center, the second two players run up and do the same thing. Play continues until the timer runs out. The team with the most points at the end wins.

Lesson: Make an outline of a boat on the floor. I used masking tape for this, but you may want to draw a boat outline on butcher paper or come up with your own idea of how to do this.

Tell students to gather around the outside of your boat.

Read Matthew 8:23-27 and have students act out the story as you read. I've given an example of how you could do this below.

"Then Jesus got into the boat, and His disciples followed Him."

Everyone, step into the boat. Remember, you have to step high to step over the side of the boat.

"Without warning, a furious storm came up on the lake..."

Everyone look furious, like you're really mad... Yeah, that's what the storm was like. Very scary.

"...so that the waves swept over the boat."

Everyone, make a big wave with your arms and make it crash over the side of the boat. Make a big splashing sound. Good.

"But Jesus was sleeping."

Everyone, pretend you're sleeping.

"The disciples went and woke him, saying, 'Lord, save us! We're going to drown!'"

Everyone, look really afraid... Good. That's probably how the disciples looked.

"Jesus replied, 'You of little faith, why are you so afraid?' Then He got up and rebuked the winds and the waves..."

Everyone, yell, "Stop!"... That's what Jesus told the storm to do. He told it to stop.

"...and it was completely calm."

Everyone, take in a deep breath. Let it out, "Ahhh!"

"The men were amazed..."

Everyone, look surprised. Yeah, it says the disciples were amazed. They were surprised that Jesus could just tell the storm what to do.

"...and asked, 'What kind of man is this? Even the winds and the waves obey Him!'"

Review Questions
How did the disciples feel when the storm came while they were in the boat? (Afraid.)

Should they have been afraid? (No.)

Why not? (Jesus was with them, and they should have known that He could help them.)

Should we ever be afraid? (No.)

We should never be afraid because we know that Jesus is with us and can help us.

If Jesus could make the storm stop and help His disciples, do you think He can help you with your problems? (Yes.)

Jesus is powerful enough to help us with any problem.

Game: Calming the Storm – Make an outline of a boat on the floor. Crumple a lot of paper. Pick a few students to stand inside the boat outline. You stand in the outline as well, pretending to be asleep. You are Jesus. They are the disciples. The rest of the students are the storm.

They pick up the crumpled papers and try to throw them into the boat outline. The disciples try to bail out their boat by removing the papers. The round ends when you yell, "Stop!" The storm stops and the disciples are able to bail out their boat.

Remind students that Jesus was able to tell the storm to stop, and it did.

Play again. This time, the students who were the disciples are now the storm, and the students who were the storm are now the disciples.

Game: Faith vs. Fear – Play the intro game again and remind students that we never need to afraid because Jesus can always help us.

Closing Prayer: Jesus, we praise You for being so powerful that You can even tell the storm to stop, and it listens to You. Help us to have faith and pray to You whenever we need help. Amen.

Recommended Extra

Jesus Stops the Storm – free coloring and activity pages

https://freesundayschoolcurriculum.weebly.com/uploads/1/2/5/0/12503916/lesson_31_jesus_stops_the_storm.pdf

Jesus Heals in Two Ways

Use this children's Sunday School lesson to teach kids how God helps us to overcome demonic influences.

Needed: Bibles, vinegar, red cabbage juice, yellow ammonia, glass, balls and "basketball hoops"

Intro Game #1: Resisting Temptation – Divide students into two teams for a slightly modified game of Red Rover. The teams line up facing each other on either side of your play area. They link hands with the students next to them.

You'll call the name of one of the students on Team A. That student must then break away from his team and try to break through the linked hands of two members of Team B. If that student breaks through, they get a point for their team. If Team B resists the charging student, Team B gets a point.

Next, call a student from Team B to try to break through Team A's line.

Play as long as time permits, alternating which team is charging and which is defending.

At the end, explain to students that a member of the opposite team is like a temptation trying to get into our hearts. The devil and the demons send temptations toward us all the time because he wants us to do something wrong. But we have to be strong and resist those temptations. We can't let them break through.

Intro Game #2 – Doctor, Doctor! – In this game of Freeze Tag, students will come to you for "healing" to get back in the game.

First, divide students into two teams. One team starts as It, chasing the other. Set a timer for 5 minutes. When a student is tagged, they have to pretend they're sick or injured and hop on one foot to where you are. You're the Doctor that can heal them. If they make it to you before they're tagged again, you can pronounce them Healed and send them back into the game as a normal player. If they get tagged before they make it to you, they're out.

The round is over when your timer goes off or when the It team tags all the members of the opposite team before they can hop over to you for healing. Have the teams switch roles and play again.

Lesson: Pour 25ml of clear vinegar into a glass. Tell students, Today, we're going to pretend that this glass is your body. And we're going to pretend that the liquid inside is your soul.

We're going to read a story today about a man who was possessed by a demon. That means a demon went into his body (pour 25ml of red cabbage juice into glass) with his soul and made the man turn dark on the inside.

But then, Jesus came and healed the man! (Pour ammonia in to fill up the rest of the glass.) The man believed in Jesus and invited God to come into His life.

The green color you see is because when we invite God to come into our lives, He makes our souls healthy and alive, like the grass that grows outside.

(Read Matthew 8:28.)

"When He arrived at the other side in the region of the Gadarenes, two demon-possessed men coming from the tombs met Him. They were so violent that no one could pass that way."

The two men were possessed by demons. What is a demon? (An evil spirit.)

17

So, an evil spirit went inside both of these men and made them go crazy and do bad things. Can a demon go inside of anybody they want to? (No.)

Demons can only go into people who don't believe in God. God protects His followers from demons. God's followers can't have demons inside them because the Holy Spirit is living inside of them, and the Holy Spirit doesn't let any demons come into you.

(Read Matthew 8:29.)

"'What do you want with us, Son of God?' they shouted. 'Have You come here to torture us before the appointed time?'"

Were these demons afraid of Jesus? (Yes.)

They asked Jesus if He was going to torture them. The demons are afraid of Jesus because they know that when Jesus comes back, He will send all of the demons to Hell and not let them bother people or go inside people anymore.

(Read Matthew 8:30-32.)

"Some distance from them a large herd of pigs was feeding. The demons begged Jesus, 'If You drive us out, send us into the herd of pigs.'

"He said to them, 'Go!' So they came out and went into the pigs, and the whole herd rushed down the steep bank into the lake and died in the water."

Jesus told the demons to come out of the men. What did the demons want to do? (They wanted to go inside some pigs.)

And Jesus told them they could go inside the pigs. Why do you think Jesus let the demons go into the pigs?

(The demons asked and Jesus was nice to them. Jesus can even be nice to the demons if He wants to be.)

But then, the demons made the pigs go crazy and run off the cliff.

(Read Matthew 8:33-34.)

"Those tending the pigs ran off, went into the town and reported all this, including what had happened to the demon-possessed men. Then the whole town went out to meet Jesus. And when they saw Him, they pleaded with Him to leave their region."

After Jesus made the demons leave the two men, it says that the people who lived in that town all asked Jesus to leave. Why do you think they asked Him to leave?

They were probably afraid of Him because He was so powerful that He could even make the demons listen to Him. They also might have been upset about that He let the demons go into the pigs and kill the pigs.

Game: Neighbors and Enemies Basketball – Set up two basketball hoops. If you don't have basketball hoops, you can use buckets, trashcans, or boxes to catch the balls. If you have a large group, you can split the students into two or more groups and set up two "baskets" for each group.

One by one, students come up to shoot two balls. They have to shoot one ball at Basket A and the other at Basket B. If they get a basket in each, they score a point. If they get a basket in only one, or neither of the baskets, they do not score a point.

Play long enough for each student to have three turns. Then, explain that Jesus wants us to be nice to our friends and our enemies because He was nice to people who believed in Him and even to the demons. If Jesus can be nice to both His friends and His enemies, then so can we.

Game: Doctor, Doctor! part 2 – Play the intro game again, but this time, have students pretend that when they are tagged, it's their spirit or soul that feels bad and that they have to come to Jesus for spiritual healing.

Explain that demons can't possess us if we believe in Jesus, but no matter what we're feeling bad about in our souls, we can still come to Jesus and have Him heal us.

Closing Prayer: Jesus, we thank You that You are able to protect and heal our souls. Help us to come to You whenever we need help. And we also pray that You'll help us to be like You and show kindness even to our enemies, just as You want us to. Amen.

Bringing Our Friends to Jesus

Use this children's Sunday School lesson to teach kids about the importance of telling others about Jesus.

Needed: Bibles, drawing paper, crayons or colored pencils

Intro Activity: Christian Story Interview – Have students pair up and ask each other the following questions. They'll then present their partner's answers as a reporter. They can write the answers down if they want.

What is your name?
How old are you?
When did you first hear about Jesus?
Who first told you about Jesus?
When was the first time you went to a church?
When was the first time you came to this church?
Why do you believe in Jesus?

After students finish presenting each other's stories, tell your own story.

Lesson: Read Matthew 9:1-2.

"Jesus stepped into a boat, crossed over and came to His own town. Some men brought to Him a paralyzed man, lying on a mat. When Jesus saw their faith, He said to the man, 'Take heart, son; your sins are forgiven.'"

What was the problem with the man in this story? (He was paralyzed. He couldn't move.)

Who brought the paralyzed man to Jesus? (Some men.)

The paralyzed man couldn't move, so he needed to have someone else bring him to Jesus. Remember that – someone had to bring the man.

What did Jesus tell the paralyzed man? ("Your sins are forgiven.")

(Read Matthew 9:3.)

"At this, some of the teachers of the law said to themselves, 'This fellow is blaspheming!'"

When Jesus said, "Your sins are forgiven," that made some people think He was blaspheming. Blaspheming is when you say wrong things about God. The people thought Jesus shouldn't have told the man his sins were forgiven because only God can forgive our sins, not regular people.

(Read Matthew 9:4-6.)

"Knowing their thoughts, Jesus said, 'Why do you entertain evil thoughts in your hearts? Which is easier: to say, "Your sins are forgiven," or to say, "Get up and walk"? But I want you to know that the Son of Man has authority on earth to forgive sins.' So he said to the paralyzed man, 'Get up, take your mat and go home.'"

Which one is easier to say, "Your sins are forgiven," or, "Get up, take your mat and go home"?

They're both pretty easy to say. But Jesus wanted people to know that He could forgive their sins, not just heal the man's body. Jesus can do both. And just like God, Jesus can forgive our sins because Jesus is part of God.

God has Three Parts: God the Father, God the Son (Jesus), and God the Holy Spirit. It's just like you have three parts: your body, your heart (emotions and mind), and your soul (spirit). Jesus could forgive sins because He was part of God.

(Read Matthew 9:7-8.)

"Then the man got up and went home. When the crowd saw this, they were filled with awe; and they praised God, who had given such authority to man."

Game: Carrying Your Friends to Jesus – Have students get into teams of five. Four friends carry the other person to the other side of the room to the leader, "Jesus." Once they get there, "Jesus" touches the person being carried and says, "You're healed." The whole team then races back to their starting line and carries another team member. The first team to bring all their friends to Jesus, get back to their line, and sit down, wins.

Tell students, Remember, the paralyzed man needed to have someone else bring Him to Jesus. He needed to have his friends bring him. And we can help bring our friends to Jesus too. We can tell our friends about Jesus and invite them to come with you to church. Inviting a friend to church is just like the paralyzed man's friends carrying him to Jesus.

Craft: Bringing Your Friends to Jesus – Give students drawing supplies and have them draw a picture of them inviting a friend to church, or having fun with their friend at church. Tell them to think of someone who doesn't already go to church.

Game: Disciple Tag – Choose one student to be It. When they tag someone, that person links hands with them and joins their team. They continue adding people to their team, linking hands with each one until all but one student is part of their chain. That remaining student becomes It for the next round.

Play two or three rounds and then, explain that when we tell people about Jesus, we want them to believe in Jesus too. If they do, they become a Christian and join our team. Then, they help us tell more people about Jesus.

Closing Prayer: Jesus, we thank You for the people who told us about You. Help us to bring others to You too. Help us tell our family members and our friends about You so that they can believe in You too. Amen.

Recommended Extra

Jesus Heals a Paralytic – free coloring and activity pages

https://freesundayschoolcurriculum.weebly.com/uploads/1/2/5/0/12503916/lesson_37_jesus_heals_a_paralytic.pdf

Jesus Helps Us If We Have Faith in Him

Use this children's Sunday School lesson to teach kids about the need to have faith in Jesus.

Needed: Bibles, Faith vs. Doubt cards, "Faith" slips of paper

Intro Game: Faith vs. Doubt – Print out or write the words Doubt or Faith on a set of index cards. You should have an equal number of cards that say Faith as Doubt.

Divide students into two teams, and have the teams line up on separate sides of the room in single file lines. Mix up the cards and give each student a card that says Faith or Doubt. Set a timer for 3-5 minutes, depending on how many students you have. When you say "Go!" the first two students run toward each and show each other their cards.

If one says Faith and the other says Doubt, the student with Faith scores a point for their team. The person with Doubt does not score. If both say Faith, both score a point and if both say Doubt, neither does. Both return to the back of their lines and trade their cards for a new card.

As soon as they leave the center, the second two players run up and do the same thing. Play continues until the timer runs out. The team with the most points at the end wins.

Lesson: Read Matthew 9:18.

"While He was saying this, a synagogue leader came and knelt before him and said, 'My daughter has just died. But come and put Your hand on her, and she will live.'"

What was the problem? (The man's daughter had just died.)

Did the man have faith that Jesus could bring his daughter back to life? (Yes.)

What is faith?

Faith is believing in something. The man had faith because He believed that Jesus could help his daughter.

(Read Matthew 9:19-21.)

"Jesus got up and went with him, and so did His disciples.

"Just then a woman who had been subject to bleeding for twelve years came up behind Him and touched the edge of His cloak. She said to herself, 'If I only touch His cloak, I will be healed.'"

What was the problem with the woman? (She had been bleeding for twelve years, and no one could help her.)

Did she have faith that Jesus could heal her? (Yes.)

(Read Matthew 9:22-24.)

"Jesus turned and saw her. 'Take heart, daughter,' He said, 'your faith has healed you.' And the woman was healed at that moment.

"When Jesus entered the synagogue leader's house and saw the noisy crowd and people playing pipes, He said, 'Go away. The girl is not dead but asleep.' But they laughed at Him."

Did the people have faith that Jesus could bring the little girl back to life? (No, they laughed at Him.)

Why do you think Jesus said the girl was asleep when she was really dead?

Being dead and being asleep is the same thing to God because He can bring someone back to life just as easily as waking someone up.

(Read Matthew 9:25-28, or read it yourself.)

"After the crowd had been put outside, He went in and took the girl by the hand, and she got up. News of this spread through all that region.

"As Jesus went on from there, two blind men followed Him, calling out, 'Have mercy on us, Son of David!'

"When He had gone indoors, the blind men came to Him, and He asked them, 'Do you believe that I am able to do this?'

"'Yes, Lord,' they replied."

What was the two men's problem? (They were blind.)

Did they have faith that Jesus could heal them? (Yes.)

(Read Matthew 9:29-32.)

"Then He touched their eyes and said, 'According to your faith let it be done to you'; and their sight was restored. Jesus warned them sternly, 'See that no one knows about this.' But they went out and spread the news about Him all over that region.

"While they were going out, a man who was demon-possessed and could not talk was brought to Jesus."

What was the man's problem? (He was possessed by a demon that made it so he couldn't talk.)

It says that someone brought the man to Jesus. If someone brought the man to Jesus, does that mean the person had faith that Jesus could help the man? (Yes.)

(Read Matthew 9:33.)

"And when the demon was driven out, the man who had been mute spoke. The crowd was amazed and said, 'Nothing like this has ever been seen in Israel.'"

Jesus healed a sick woman who couldn't stop bleeding for 12 years, He brought a dead little girl back to life, healed two blind men, and a demon-possessed man who couldn't talk. What did each of those people have to do for Jesus to help them? (They had to have faith that Jesus could help them.)

Do you have faith that Jesus can help you with your problems? (Yes.)

Jesus can help us with any problem we have. It doesn't have to be just when we're sick. Jesus doesn't help us the way we want Him to all the time, but if we want Jesus to help us, we need to have faith.

How can you ask Jesus to help you? (Pray.)

You can pray and ask for Jesus' help whenever you want to, wherever you are, and He will hear you.

Game: Finding Faith – Before class, hide strips of paper around the room with the word "Faith" written on them. Then, divide students into two or more teams. When you say, "Go!" the team members search the room to find the slips of paper. Once someone finds a slip of paper, they return to their team's starting area and wait for the others to find theirs. The first team to have all their members find a slip of paper and make it to their team's starting area wins.

When the game is finished, remind students that we all need to have faith, and we all need to have our own faith, if we want Jesus to help us.

Game: Heal Tag – Pick 2-4 students to be It. When they tag someone that person must freeze and pretend to be the dead girl, the sick woman, the blind man, or the man who couldn't talk by acting out these characters as best they can. Other players can be "Jesus" and go tag them to unfreeze (heal) them.

Closing Prayer: Jesus, we thank You that You can help us no matter what problem we have. Help us to have faith in You. Amen.

Recommended Extra

Jesus Makes a Dead Girl Live – free coloring and activity pages

https://freesundayschoolcurriculum.weebly.com/uploads/1/2/5/0/12503916/lesson_39_jesus_makes_a_dead_girl_live.pdf

Jesus Brings a Dead Boy Back to Life!

Use this children's Sunday School lesson to teach kids that Jesus has the power over death.

Needed: Bibles

Intro Game: Get Up! – Have students lie down on the floor. Sitting is fine if you don't have enough room for everyone to lie down. When you yell, "Get up!" everyone should get to their feet and jump into the air as quickly as they can. The first person to jump gets to be the next caller. Play as long as time allows. Be sure to give everyone a chance to be the caller, even if you have to ask someone who's already done it to give up their turn.

Lesson: Ask students, How many of you know someone who has died? Who was it?

It's very sad when someone dies, but I have some good news for you today.

(Read Luke 7:11-12.)

"Soon afterward, Jesus went to a town called Nain, and His disciples and a large crowd went along with Him. As He approached the town gate, a dead person was being carried out—the only son of his mother, and she was a widow. And a large crowd from the town was with her."

What bad thing happened in this story? (A woman's son died.)

How do you think the woman felt when her son died? (Sad.)

(Read Luke 7:13.)

"When the Lord saw her, His heart went out to her and He said, 'Don't cry.'"

When Jesus saw the mother and the people carrying the dead son, how did Jesus feel? (He felt bad for the mother.)

Do you think Jesus feels bad for you when something bad happens to you? (Yes.)

Jesus loves you and cares about you and doesn't want to see bad things happen to you.

(Read Luke 7:14-15.)

"Then He went up and touched the bier they were carrying him on, and the bearers stood still. He said, 'Young man, I say to you, get up!' The dead man sat up and began to talk, and Jesus gave him back to his mother."

What did Jesus do for the mother whose son had died? (Jesus brought the son back to life.)

Someday, Jesus will come back to Earth and He will bring everyone who believes in Him back to life who has died, and He will make it so that everyone who hasn't died and believes in Him will never die. He'll make our bodies perfect so that we can't get sick, or get hurt, or get old anymore. And we will all live with Jesus and God forever.

Game: Get Up! – Play the intro game again and remind students that Jesus will tell us all to get up and come back to life one day, just like he told the dead boy to get up and brought him back to life.

Game: Resurrection Tag – Pick one student to be It. That student is Death. Pick another student to be Jesus. When Death tags someone, they fall down and lie on the ground like they're dead. Jesus can then come to tag them, and they can get back up. If Death tags Jesus, Jesus must count to three (because

Jesus was dead for three days), but can then get up again. If Jesus tags Death, the round is over. Play until everyone has had a chance to be both Death and Jesus or as long as time permits.

Remind students that Jesus will come back one day and will raise everyone who believes in Him back to life.

Closing Prayer: Jesus, we thank You for caring about us, and we thank You that You will bring all of us back to life if we believe in You. Help us to believe in You until You come. Amen.

Recommended Extras

Jesus Raises a Widow's Son – free coloring and activity pages

> https://freesundayschoolcurriculum.weebly.com/uploads/1/2/5/0/12503916/lesson_35_jesus_raises_a_widows_son.pdf

A Miraculous Turnaround – free object lesson, along with free coloring and activity pages

> https://www.sermons4kids.com/miraculous_turnaround.htm

The Proof of Who Jesus Is

Use this children's Sunday School lesson to show that Jesus proved who He said He was by what He did and that we need to prove we're His followers by what we do.

Needed: Bibles, various snacks or challenges in paper bags, drawing paper, crayons or colored pencils

Intro Game: Eat It! – Before class, place various food or beverage items in individual paper bags. Close the bags and line them up on a table. Suggestions include a bottle of water, a cookie, a piece of fruit, a package of crackers, a juice box, etc.

Divide the students into two teams. Call the first student from each team forward and set the first bag in front of them. Do not show them what's in the bag. Tell them that if they can eat what is in the bag in a certain time limit, they'll get a point for their team. But only one of them will get a chance to eat it. If the person eating it can't finish it within the time limit, the other team gets a point.

Start the time limit at 1 minute and ask the player from Team A if they can eat what's in the bag within 1 minute. If they say they can, ask the player from B how fast they can eat it. The two players each take turns reducing the time until one of them doesn't think they can eat it faster than the other. At that point, they challenge their opponent to eat it within the time limit by saying "Prove it."

Award the point based on whether the player eats or drinks the item in the specified time limit. Then, call the next two players up and start again, this time starting with the player from Team B.

Play until all students have had a chance to participate.

Alternative: Instead of food items in the bag, you could have slips of paper with challenges written on them, such as "Do 10 jumping jacks" or "Find the Book of Job."

Lesson: Ask students, If I said I was God, would you believe me?

What would I have to do to prove to you that I was God?

Well, I'm not God, of course, but Jesus was. Jesus is God in a human body. And it was hard for people to believe that He was God too. Even John the Baptist wasn't totally sure.

(Read Matthew 11:2-6, or read it yourself.)

"When John, who was in prison, heard about the deeds of the Messiah, he sent his disciples to ask Him, 'Are you the one who is to come, or should we expect someone else?'

"Jesus replied, 'Go back and report to John what you hear and see: The blind receive sight, the lame walk, those who have leprosy are cleansed, the deaf hear, the dead are raised, and the good news is proclaimed to the poor. Blessed is anyone who does not stumble on account of Me.'"

When John sent someone to ask Jesus if He was really the Savior, Jesus told John how he could know. He said, "My proof that I'm the Savior is that I can make blind people see. I can make people who can't walk, walk. I can heal people's diseases and make deaf people hear. I can bring dead people back to life, and I preach about God to everyone, even the poor people who no one else cares about."

Jesus was telling John that no one else could do the miracles that He was doing. And because Jesus could do those things, that proves that He is the Savior and that He is God.

And because Jesus is the Savior and God, we can have faith in Him.

Game: Jesus' Miracles Relay – Divide students into two or more teams. When you say, "Go!" the first student on each team will perform the first leg of the relay race, acting out the first motion as they travel to the other side of your play area, and acting out the second motion as they run back to their team. The second student on each team then does the second leg, and so on until that team completes the last leg. The first team to complete all legs of the race wins.

Leg 1. The Blind. Cover one eye, then run with both eyes open to show that Jesus healed the blind.

Leg 2. The Lame. Hop on one foot, then run to show that Jesus healed the lame.

Leg 3. The Leprous. Scratch your skin, then run normally.

Leg 4. The Deaf. Put your hands over your ears, then run normally.

Leg 5. The Dead. Hold your hands over your chest and walk backward, then run forward to show that Jesus raised the dead.

Leg 6. The Poor. Hold your hands out like you're begging, then run with your arms up to show that Jesus gave the poor good news.

Craft: The Proof is in the Action – Give students drawing supplies and say something like, Jesus showed that He was the Savior and God by what He did. We prove that we're Jesus' followers by what we do. Draw a picture of you doing something that proves that You're one of Jesus' followers.

Closing Prayer: Jesus, we know You are who You say You are because of what You did. Help us to prove that we're Your followers by what we do. Amen.

When are We Allowed to Break the Rules?

Use this children's Sunday School lesson to help students understand the need to do the best thing over the good thing.

Needed: Bibles, cookies or other small prizes

Intro Activity: Acting It Out – Divide students into groups of three or four. Have each group decide on and act out one part of your church service. After each group, briefly discuss why your church includes that in its weekly worship. Point out that doing those actions are part of the way you make the Sabbath a holy day.

Intro Game: Good vs. Best – For this game show type game, you'll call on volunteers to come up and answer a question about the Bible (choose questions you think kids will know). If they get the answer right, give them a cookie or other small prize. Then, tell them that they can take their one cookie or prize and sit down or they can try to answer another question. If they get the second question right, they'll get a second cookie or an even better prize. If they get it wrong, they lose their cookie or prize they earned from answering the first question.

When everyone who wants to has had a chance to play, ask, Was it a difficult choice deciding if you were going to try to answer the second question? Why or why not?

Sometimes, we need to make difficult decisions, and we have to think about what the best choice is.

http://www.dltk-bible.com/quiz.htm

Lesson: Ask students, What are some rules you have in your house?

Are you ever allowed to break those rules?

What if one of the rules in your house is that you're not allowed to run in the house, but then a fire starts in your house; are you allowed to run away from the fire even if that means you have to run in the house? (Yes.)

Your parents don't want you to run in the house usually because you might bump into something or fall and hurt yourself. But if there's a fire, then they would want you to break the rule so that you could get away and be safe. It's the choice between doing the good thing of not running and the best thing of running in that situation.

What if it was your bedtime and you were supposed to be in bed, but then you heard your mom or dad fall down; are you allowed to get up and go see if they're okay even though you're supposed to be in bed? (Yes.)

Your parents usually want you to stay in bed when it's bedtime, but if they fall down and get hurt, they would like it if you came to help them. It's the choice between doing the good thing of staying in bed and the best thing of going to check on your parents.

So, there are times when we're allowed to break the rules if we're trying to do something more important than following the rules, like getting away from a fire or making sure our parents are okay.

It's the same way with God's rules.

(Read Matthew 12:1-2.)

"At that time Jesus went through the grainfields on the Sabbath. His disciples were hungry and began to pick some heads of grain and eat them. When the Pharisees saw this, they said to Him, 'Look! Your disciples are doing what is unlawful on the Sabbath.'"

Jesus' disciples were hungry and were picking food out of the farm field and eating it. But the Pharisees said the disciples were breaking the rules because you weren't supposed to be doing farm work on the Sabbath. God's rule was that the Sabbath day was only for going to church and resting.

(Read Matthew 12:3-8.)

"He answered, 'Haven't you read what David did when he and his companions were hungry? He entered the house of God, and he and his companions ate the consecrated bread—which was not lawful for them to do, but only for the priests. Or haven't you read in the Law that the priests on Sabbath duty in the temple desecrate the Sabbath and yet are innocent? I tell you that something greater than the temple is here. If you had known what these words mean, "I desire mercy, not sacrifice," you would not have condemned the innocent. For the Son of Man is Lord of the Sabbath.'"

Jesus said that sometimes there are special reasons why it's okay to break God's rules.

(Read Matthew 12:9-10.)

"Going on from that place, He went into their synagogue, and a man with a shriveled hand was there. Looking for a reason to bring charges against Jesus, they asked Him, 'Is it lawful to heal on the Sabbath?'"

One day, when Jesus went to church, he saw a man whose hand didn't work right. The Pharisees said it was against the rules for Jesus to heal the man's hand because it was the Sabbath day, and God's rule was that you weren't allowed to work on the Sabbath day. The Sabbath day was only supposed to be for going to church and resting.

But do you think God would want Jesus to heal the man's hand, even if that meant breaking the rules and doing a little bit of work on the Sabbath? (Yes.)

God likes it when we help other people, and God wanted Jesus to heal the man's hand, even if that meant breaking the rule of the Sabbath.

(Read Matthew 12:11-12.)

"He said to them, 'If any of you has a sheep and it falls into a pit on the Sabbath, will you not take hold of it and lift it out? How much more valuable is a person than a sheep! Therefore it is lawful to do good on the Sabbath.'"

Jesus said it was okay to help the man because it was a good thing to do to help the man, even if that meant breaking the rule about not doing any work on the Sabbath. Jesus knew God would want Him to break the rules if He had a good enough reason, just like your parents would want you to break the rules in your house if you had a good enough reason.

Jesus had the choice between doing the good thing of keeping the Sabbath and the best thing of helping the man with the disabled hand.

(Read Matthew 12:13.)

"Then He said to the man, 'Stretch out your hand.' So he stretched it out and it was completely restored, just as sound as the other."

Game: Hide and Go Sheep – Pick one person to be It. They are the Shepherd. Everyone else is the Sheep. They go and hide while the Shepherd counts. The Shepherd then tries to find the Sheep. When he or she finds one, that Sheep helps them look for the others. The last Sheep found becomes the new Shepherd for the next round. Play as long as time allows or until everyone has had a chance to be the Shepherd.

Remind students that just like the Shepherd goes to find his sheep that need help, so Jesus helps us.

Closing Prayer: Jesus, we pray that You'll give us wisdom always to do the right thing, even if it means breaking other good rules. Amen.

Recommended Extra

Jesus Heals a Man's Hand – free coloring and activity pages

https://freesundayschoolcurriculum.weebly.com/uploads/1/2/5/0/12503916/lesson_27_jesus_heals_a_mans_hand.pdf

Jesus Takes Our Little and Makes it A Lot – Feeding the Five Thousand

Use this children's Sunday School lesson to teach kids how Jesus uses what we give Him to help others.

Needed: Bibles, strips of paper, snack

Intro Game: Delivering the Fish and Loaves – Divide students into two or teams for a relay race. Place a pile of paper strips at the other end of the play area in front of each team.

The first student from each team runs down to the pile, grabs a slip of paper, and hands it to the next person in line, who then does the same thing. The team continues running until each team member has retrieved and is holding a slip of paper. The first team to finish wins.

Snack Activity: No Leftovers?! - Bring a snack in to share with the class. It could be anything – pretzels, candy, fruit cups, doughnuts, etc.

Before passing the snack out, ask students, If I give you all of this snack, will I have any leftover? (No. If you give it all to the students, you won't have any leftover.)

Okay. Well, I'll give you all some of the snack, anyway.

(Pass out the snack and let children eat. When they're finished, tell them to pass in their leftovers. They won't have any.)

You mean you ate the snack and don't have any leftovers? Well, this is not the way it happened in the Bible. Let's read a story about a time when Jesus gave people a snack and had lots left over.

Lesson: Read John 6:1-15.

"Some time after this, Jesus crossed to the far shore of the Sea of Galilee (that is, the Sea of Tiberias), and a great crowd of people followed Him because they saw the signs He had performed by healing the sick. Then Jesus went up on a mountainside and sat down with His disciples. The Jewish Passover Festival was near.

"When Jesus looked up and saw a great crowd coming toward Him, He said to Philip, 'Where shall we buy bread for these people to eat?' He asked this only to test him, for he already had in mind what He was going to do.

"Philip answered Him, 'It would take more than half a year's wages to buy enough bread for each one to have a bite!'

"Another of His disciples, Andrew, Simon Peter's brother, spoke up, 'Here is a boy with five small barley loaves and two small fish, but how far will they go among so many?'

"Jesus said, 'Have the people sit down.' There was plenty of grass in that place, and they sat down (about five thousand men were there). Jesus then took the loaves, gave thanks, and distributed to those who were seated as much as they wanted. He did the same with the fish.

"When they had all had enough to eat, He said to His disciples, 'Gather the pieces that are left over. Let nothing be wasted.' So they gathered them and filled twelve baskets with the pieces of the five barley loaves left over by those who had eaten.

"After the people saw the sign Jesus performed, they began to say, 'Surely this is the Prophet who is to come into the world.' Jesus, knowing that they intended to come and make Him king by force, withdrew again to a mountain by Himself."

How many people were there in the crowd? (5,000 men, plus women and children.)

How much food did Jesus have? (5 loaves of bread and 2 fish.)

Can 5 loaves of bread and 2 fish feed more than 5,000 people? (No.)

Then, how did Jesus feed them all? (He did a miracle to make more food out of the 5 loaves and 2 fish.)

And then, the Bible says that Jesus still had leftovers afterward.

He started with 5 loaves of bread and 2 fish, fed more than 5,000 people, and ended up with more food than He started with!

This is still what Jesus does for us. The boy gave Jesus what he had. It was just a little bit, but Jesus was able to make more out of it. If we give what we have to Jesus, even if it's just a little bit, He can use it in great ways.

Let's think of some things that we can give to Jesus.

What can you give Jesus? (Suggestions include money in the offering, giving our time and talents to Jesus by helping at church or helping other people, giving Jesus our hearts when we love Him and do what He says, etc.)

(Teachers should also share how they give and help in the church, including teaching.)

When we give what we have to Jesus, we have faith that He can use it to help other people, just like Jesus used the boy's 5 loaves and 2 fish.

Game: Delivering the Fish and Loaves – Play the intro game again, but this time, tell students that they're like the disciples handing out the food from Jesus to all the people.

Closing Prayer: Jesus, we give You everything that we have and pray that You'll use it to help others as only You can. Amen.

Recommended Extras

Jesus Feeds 5,000 – free coloring and activity pages

> https://freesundayschoolcurriculum.weebly.com/uploa ds/1/2/5/0/12503916/lesson_44_jesus_feeds_5000.pdf

Feeding the 5,000 – free object lesson, along with free coloring and activity pages

> https://www.sermons4kids.com/feeding_the_five_thou sand.htm

Faith, Not Fear – Jesus Walks On the Water

Use this children's Sunday School lesson to teach kids that we never need to be afraid if we have faith in Jesus.

Needed: Bibles, kiddie pool or basin, various sinkable and unsinkable objects, Faith vs. Fear cards, playing cards or UNO cards of Go Fish! cards

Intro Activity: Will It Float? - Fill up a kiddie pool or large basin with water. Gather various objects, including some that will float and some that will not. Have kids guess if an object will float or sink and then, drop it in the water to see what happens. End by asking if a human would float or sink.

Take off your shoes and then step in to demonstrate.

Students may step in with your permission.

Lesson: Well, we couldn't float on the water, but we're going to read a story today about Someone who could.

(Read Matthew 14:22-27.)

"Immediately Jesus made the disciples get into the boat and go on ahead of Him to the other side, while he dismissed the crowd. After He had dismissed them, He went up on a mountainside by Himself to pray. Later that night, He was there alone, and the boat was already a considerable distance from land, buffeted by the waves because the wind was against it.

"Shortly before dawn Jesus went out to them, walking on the lake. When the disciples saw Him walking on the lake, they were terrified. 'It's a ghost,' they said, and cried out in fear.

"But Jesus immediately said to them: 'Take courage! It is I. Don't be afraid.'"

How could Jesus walk on the water? (It was a miracle that God gave Him the power to do.)

When the disciples were afraid and thought that He was a ghost, what did Jesus say to them? (He told them not to be afraid.)

Do you think God ever wants you to be afraid? (No.)

God never wants us to be afraid. We don't have to be afraid because we know God is always with us and will help us.

(Read Matthew 14:28-31.)

"'Lord, if it's you,' Peter replied, 'tell me to come to You on the water.'

"'Come,' He said.

"Then Peter got down out of the boat, walked on the water and came toward Jesus. But when he saw the wind, he was afraid and, beginning to sink, cried out, 'Lord, save me!'

"Immediately Jesus reached out His hand and caught him. 'You of little faith,' He said, 'why did you doubt?'

Why did Peter start to sink? (Because he got scared.)

Should be Peter have been scared? (No. Jesus was with him.)

What did Jesus say that Peter had little of? (Faith.)

Jesus said Peter had only a little faith. If Peter had had a lot of faith in Jesus, he wouldn't have been afraid. Do you have enough faith in Jesus not to be afraid when something happens to you?

(Read Matthew 14:32-36.)

"And when they climbed into the boat, the wind died down. Then those who were in the boat worshiped him, saying, 'Truly you are the Son of God.'

"When they had crossed over, they landed at Gennesaret. And when the men of that place recognized Jesus, they sent word to all the surrounding country. People brought all their sick to Him and begged Him to let the sick just touch the edge of His cloak, and all who touched it were healed."

Game: Faith vs. Fear – Print out or write the words Fear or Faith on a set of index cards. You should have an equal number of cards that say Faith as Fear.

Divide students into two teams, and have the teams line up on separate sides of the room in single file lines. Mix up the cards and give each student a card that says Faith or Fear. Set a timer for 3-5 minutes, depending on how many students you have. When you say Go! the first two students run toward each and show each other their cards.

If one says Faith and the other says Fear, the student with Faith scores a point for their team. The person with Fear does not score. If both say Faith, both score a point and if both say Fear, neither does. Both return to the back of their lines and trade their cards for a new card.

As soon as they leave the center, the second two players run up and do the same thing. Play continues until the timer runs out. The team with the most points at the end wins.

Game: Fast Reflexes – Lay out a deck of game cards on a table, face up. The cards could be regular playing cards, UNO cards, Go Fish! cards, etc.

Students gather around the table. You'll call out a type of card (a number, color, shape, etc.). The last student to reach out and touch that type of card is out.

The last student in the game wins and becomes the caller for the next round.

Remind students that when Peter was sinking, he called out for Jesus to help him, and Jesus immediately reached out for him. Jesus does the same for us. When we pray to Him for help, He helps us very quickly and always in the best way. It's just that sometimes, Jesus doesn't help us the way we want Him to help us. He helps us in the way that will be best for us.

Closing Prayer: Jesus, we pray that You'll help us to have faith in You and know that we don't need ever need to be afraid because You're always with us. Amen.

Recommended Extras

Jesus Walks on Water – free coloring and activity pages

> https://freesundayschoolcurriculum.weebly.com/uploads/1/2/5/0/12503916/lesson_45_jesus_walks_on_water.pdf

Walkin' on the Water – free object lesson, along with free coloring and activity pages

> https://www.sermons4kids.com/walk_on_water.htm

The Faith of a Foreign Enemy – The Faith of a Canaanite Woman

Use this children's Sunday School lesson to teach kids to be humble in their faith and not to judge anyone.

Needed: Bibles, a small ball or paper wad, strips of paper with "Faith" written on them

Intro Game: Dogs and Leftovers – Choose one student to be the Master. They turn around with the rest of the students behind them. They then throw a ball or paper wad (their Leftovers) over their head behind them.

The rest of the students are the Dogs who try to catch the Leftovers. The student who catches the ball or picks it up then has to run from the rest of the Dogs to keep their prize.

If they make it in front of the Master, they're safe and become the new Master. If another Dog tags them, they're out of the game, and the Dog who tagged them becomes the new Master.

Lesson: Ask students, Does our country have any enemies? Are there any other countries that we're fighting with?

What about you? Do you have any enemies? Is there anyone at school that you really don't like, or who you fight with a lot?

(Read Matthew 15:21-22.)

"Leaving that place, Jesus withdrew to the region of Tyre and Sidon. A Canaanite woman from that vicinity came to Him, crying out, 'Lord, Son of David, have mercy on me! My daughter is demon-possessed and suffering terribly.'"

What kind of woman was she? (A Canaanite.)

Canaanites were old enemies of the Jewish people. Most Jewish people, like Jesus' disciples, wouldn't have liked this woman because she was a Canaanite.

What did the woman want help with? (She wanted Jesus to heal her daughter, who was demon-possessed.)

Do you think Jesus will help the woman, even though she's a Canaanite?

(Read Matthew 15:23-24.)

"Jesus did not answer a word. So His disciples came to Him and urged Him, 'Send her away, for she keeps crying out after us.'

"He answered, "I was sent only to the lost sheep of Israel.'"

Why didn't Jesus help the woman? (He said He was only sent to help Jewish people. He wasn't supposed to help Canaanites.)

Do you think Jesus should help the woman, anyway? Why or why not?

(Read Matthew 15:25-26.)

"The woman came and knelt before Him. 'Lord, help me!' she said.

"He replied, 'It is not right to take the children's bread and toss it to the dogs.'"

Why did Jesus call the woman a dog? (Because she was a Canaanite, an enemy of the Jewish people, and didn't deserve to have Jesus help her.)

(Read Matthew 15:27.)

"'Yes it is, Lord,' she said. 'Even the dogs eat the crumbs that fall from their master's table.'"

What did the woman call herself? (A dog.)

The woman was saying that she knew she didn't deserve to have Jesus help her. And the thing we have to remember is that none of us deserve to have Jesus help us, either. God doesn't have to do anything for us.

He doesn't owe us anything. So, we're all like that woman. None of us deserve to have Jesus do anything for us.

(Read Matthew 15:28.)

"Then Jesus said to her, 'Woman, you have great faith! Your request is granted.' And her daughter was healed at that moment."

Why did Jesus finally help the woman? (Because she had great faith.)

Jesus helped the woman because she had faith in Him.

She believed in Him. That shows us that anyone can have faith in Jesus, even people who are supposed to be our enemies, like the Canaanite woman was supposed to be Jesus' enemy because Jesus was Jewish. But anyone can believe in Jesus, no matter where they're from or what the rest of the people in their country are like.

And we can believe in Jesus too. We can have great faith, just like the Canaanite woman did.

So let's remember three things today:

1. None of us deserve to have God do anything for us.

2. Anyone can believe in Jesus, no matter who they are.

3. Jesus wants us all to have great faith, like the Canaanite woman did.

If we all have great faith like the Canaanite woman did, then God will be happy with us for believing in Him.

Prayer Activity: Humble Gratitude – Have kids spread out around the room and pray silently. Direct them to think about all the ways God has helped them, including sending Jesus to take the punishment for their sins.

Then, have them acknowledge to God that they didn't deserve His help.

Finally, have them thank Him for helping them in all the ways they listed even though they didn't deserve it.

Remind students that God and Jesus help us because they love us.

Game: Finding Faith – Before class, hide strips of paper around the room with the word "Faith" written on them. Then, divide students into two or more teams. When you say, "Go!" the team members search the room to find the slips of paper. Once someone finds a slip of paper, they return to their team's starting area and wait for the others to find theirs. The first team to have all their members find a slip of paper and make it to their team's starting area wins.

When the game is finished, remind students that we all need to have faith, just like the Canaanite woman did, if we want Jesus to help us.

Game: Dogs and Leftovers – Play the intro game again and remind students of how the woman was humble when she asked Jesus to help her.

Closing Prayer: Jesus, thank You for everything that You do for us. Help us to be humble like the Canaanite woman was and help us to remember that anyone can have faith in You, no matter who they are.

Recommended Extra

Crumbs from the Table – free object lesson, along with free coloring and activity pages

https://www.sermons4kids.com/crumbs.html

Jesus Heals a Blind Man - Twice!

Use this children's Sunday School lesson to teach kids that God doesn't usually help us with all of our problems at one time.

Needed: Bibles, various items around the room

Intro Game #1: Two for Two – Divide students into two teams and ask the questions below. The first team to shout the answer gets a point. The team with the most points at the end wins.

1. What happens twice a day? (The clock reads the same time.)
2. What two body parts do people see with? (Eyes.)
3. What two body parts do people walk with? (Legs.)
4. What two body parts do people walk on? (Feet.)
5. What two body parts do people hear with? (Ears.)
6. What two body parts do people filter their blood with? (Kidneys.)
7. What two body parts do people pick things up with? (Hands.)
8. What two body parts do people breathe with? (Nostrils or lungs.)

Intro Game #2: Find a Pair – Name an item around your room that matches another item in some way (color, shape, identical match, etc.). The first student to bring you the matching item wins and gest to name the next item.

Lesson: Ask students, When we believe in Jesus, does that make all of our problems go away?

What if God did something for us and answered one of our prayers; would that mean that God was answering all of our prayers?

(Read Mark 8:22-26.)

"They came to Bethsaida, and some people brought a blind man and begged Jesus to touch him. He took the blind man by the hand and led him outside the village. When He had spit on the man's eyes and put His hands on him, Jesus asked, 'Do you see anything?'

"He looked up and said, 'I see people; they look like trees walking around.'

"Once more Jesus put His hands on the man's eyes. Then his eyes were opened, his sight was restored, and he saw everything clearly. Jesus sent him home, saying, 'Don't even go into the village.'"

How many times did Jesus have to touch the man's eyes before he could see perfectly? (Twice.)

Jesus touched the man's eyes once, and he could see a little better, but he said that people looked like trees.

Then, Jesus touched his eyes again, and he could see perfectly.

Jesus didn't heal the man completely the first time Jesus touched him. Jesus touched him twice. That's like how sometimes, God doesn't make all of our problems go away at once. Sometimes, God helps things get a little bit better, but then, He waits to make them all the way better. Or sometimes, God will do one thing that we asked Him to do, but then, He'll wait a little while before He does the other thing we asked Him to do.

So, remember, God usually doesn't take away all of our problems at once. He does it little by little and sometimes, it takes a long time for God to help us with everything we need help with, but He will eventually help us. We just have to be patient.

Game: Tilly Miller – Tell students that Tilly Miller likes balloons and balls, but she doesn't like toys. Ask them why. If they can't get the reason (and they probably won't unless they've heard this before), keep telling them things that Tilly Miller likes and doesn't like. For example, she likes fluffy cotton candy and taffy, but she doesn't like gumballs or candy bars.

The trick is that Tilly Miller likes anything that has double letters and nothing that doesn't have double letters. To help kids get the answer, you can write out what she likes and doesn't like.

When one of the students figure out the answer, remind them God doesn't always help us with everything all at once. Sometimes, He wants to help us with different things at different times.

Closing Prayer: Jesus, we thank You for always caring about us and wanting to help us. We pray that You'll help us to be patient as You work with us and help us as quickly or as slowly as You want to, all at once or a little bit a time, just like You did with the blind man in the story. Amen.

Jesus Heals a Man Born Blind

Use this children's Sunday School lesson to teach kids that bad things don't always happen as a punishment from God and that we need to be faithful to God even when others tell us we shouldn't or aren't allowed to.

Needed: Bibles, a volunteer to play blind man (You can do this yourself if you want.), blindfolds, writing or drawing paper, pencils or pens and crayons or colored pencils

Intro Game: Blindfold Challenge –Have the students pair up in a safe area. One of the students will put on a blindfold. The other will give them verbal directions of where to go. When I used this game, I had the children lead each other to another room in the church. You could also take the kids outside to walk a path around your property or set up a course for them to follow in your classroom.

Once they get to the ending location, have them switch. The one giving directions will now take their blindfolded partner to a third location or back to the classroom via a different route.

Ask children, Was it difficult to move when you were pretending you were blind?

Were you afraid you might trip into something or bump into something?

If you were blind, would you want Jesus to heal you?

Lesson: Read John 9 or summarize it with the following script.

Blind Man: Hi, everyone! I want to tell you about the time I met Jesus. I was a blind man. I had always been blind, even when I was first born. One day, Jesus and His disciples were walking along, and they saw me.

Jesus' disciples asked Him what bad thing I had done or what bad thing my parents had done for God to make me blind like that. But Jesus said I wasn't blind because God was punishing me. I was blind because God wanted to do a miracle for me! Then, Jesus spit on the dirt, made some mud, and put the mud on my eyes. "Go wash off," He told me, and when I washed the mud off, I could see! I wasn't blind anymore.

I went home, and all of my neighbors were amazed that I could see. I told them that Jesus did it, and then, they took me to the Pharisees so that I could tell them too. But the Pharisees said Jesus was bad because He had healed me on the Sabbath, and we're not supposed to work on the Sabbath. We're only supposed to go to church and rest on the Sabbath. They said I was lying because they didn't think Jesus was a good man and that He could heal me as He did.

The Pharisees made my parents come to talk to them, but my parents didn't know what to say. They didn't want to tell the Pharisees that Jesus healed me because the Pharisees said they would kick anyone out of the church if they believed in Jesus.

I told the Pharisees again that Jesus must be a good man that came from God for God to give Him the power to heal me, but they still didn't believe me and kicked me out of the church.

A little while later, Jesus came and found me again. He asked me if I believed in Him. I said that I did and then, I bowed down and worshipped Him. Then, He said that *my* eyes had been blind, but that it was the *Pharisees* who couldn't see the truth because they were the ones who wouldn't believe in Him like God wanted them to.

Do you all believe in Jesus?

That's good. Because Jesus said that if we believe in Him, then God forgives us for all the wrong things we've done.

Well, goodbye!

(Have students thank the blind man for coming.)

Review Questions
How long had the man been blind? (His whole life, since he was born.)

Was the man blind because he had something wrong? Did his parents do something wrong? Did God make the man blind as a punishment? (No.)

What did the Pharisees do to the man because He believed in Jesus? (They kicked him out of the church.)

It was against the law back then to believe in Jesus, and in some countries, it's still against the law to believe in Jesus. People get put in jail and even killed if they believe in Jesus. But the man was brave to believe in Jesus anyway, even if he did get in trouble and get kicked out of the church because of it.

What did Jesus say we had to do for God to forgive us for our sins? (We have to believe in Jesus.)

Game: Pass it On – Have students sit in a line or a circle, holding hands with the person next to them.

Have them all close their eyes. The leader should be on the end with their own eyes open. The leader will squeeze the hand of the person next to them. That person will open their eyes and then squeeze the hand of the third person.

So, when a person feels their hand being squeezed, they should open their eyes and then, pass the squeeze on. The goal of the game is for everyone to open their eyes, going down the line or around the circle, as fast as possible. Play a couple of times to get your speed up. Feel free to rotate who starts the line or circle.

Tell students, When we believe in Jesus, it's like our eyes are being opened, and we can see the truth. And if we believe in Jesus and can see the truth, then it's our job to tell other people about Jesus so that they can believe in Jesus and see the truth too, just like how we passed our hand-squeeze down the line today.

Craft: The Persecuted Church – Look up a current news story about where Christians are being persecuted. Show the location on a map and summarize the situation for the children and explain why a certain government doesn't want the people to believe in God. Then, have students write a prayer for their fellow Christians in that situation, or draw a picture illustrating God's protection around those persecuted Christians.

https://www.opendoorsusa.org/

Closing Prayer: Jesus, we thank You for helping us to see clearly who You are. We pray that You'll keep us faithful to You even when other people don't believe in You or say that we're not allowed to believe in You. We pray that You'll be with all the people who are being persecuted right now because they believe in You. Amen.

Recommended Extras

Jesus Heals a Man Born Blind – free coloring and activity pages

https://freesundayschoolcurriculum.weebly.com/uploads/1/2/5/0/12503916/lesson_23_jesus_heals_a_man_born_blind.pdf

Here's Mud in Your Eye – free object lesson, along with free coloring and activity pages https://www.sermons4kids.com/mud_in_your_eye.htm

The Transfiguration – Jesus is Most Important

Use this children's Sunday School lesson to teach kids the importance of obeying Jesus.

Needed: Bibles, a volunteer to play Peter (You can do this yourself if you want.), playing cards of UNO cards or Go Fish! cards

Lesson: Read Matthew 17:1-9 or summarize it with the following script.

Peter: Hi, friends! I'm Peter. I was one of Jesus' disciples, and I want to tell you about a very strange time we had with Jesus. You see, one day, Jesus took James, John, and I up a high mountain. It was just the four of us.

And when we got to the top of the mountain, Jesus changed right before our eyes. His face started shining like the sun, and His clothes became bright white.

And then, Moses and the prophet Elijah were there with Jesus, talking to Him about how He was going to die on the cross soon.

I told them I would build them all churches up there, but that was a silly idea.

Then, a cloud came and covered the top of the mountain where we were. We were in the cloud, and we heard God's voice. He said, "Jesus is My Son. I love Him, and I am happy with Him. Do what He says!" James, John, and I were so scared that we bowed down to the ground and wouldn't look up.

Then, Jesus came and touched us. He said, "Get up. Don't be afraid." We looked up, and it was all over. The cloud was gone,

Moses and Elijah had gone back up to Heaven, and Jesus looked like His normal self again.

That was a strange day, but it definitely taught us a lot about how great Jesus really is.

Well, thanks for letting me come talk to you. Goodbye!

(Have students thank Peter for coming.)

Review Questions
Who came down from Heaven to visit Jesus? (Moses and Elijah.)

Who was Moses in the Bible? (Moses led the Israelites out of slavery in Egypt and gave the Israelites the Ten Commandments and the rest of God's rules. He even wrote the first five books of the Bible.)

Who was Elijah in the Bible? (Elijah was the first prophet for God. When Israel started worshipping other gods, he preached and reminded the Israelites and their bad kings to worship God and to do the right things that God wanted them to do.)

Do you remember what God called Jesus when God was talking in the cloud? (God called Jesus His Son.)

So, Moses and Elijah and Jesus were all great leaders who served God, but Jesus was the most important out of all of them because He was God's Son. Moses and Elijah were regular humans, but Jesus was God's very own Son, and that made Jesus very special.

Does anyone remember what God told the disciples to do? (God told the disciples to listen to Jesus and to do what Jesus told them.)

And that's what God wants us to do too. He wants us to listen to Jesus and to what He tells us. If we believe in Jesus and listen to Him, then God will be happy with us, just like He was happy with Jesus.

So, remember, Jesus is the most important person because He's God's very own Son, and God wants us to listen to Him and do everything that He tells us.

Game: Jesus Says – In this game of Simon Says, students follow your commands and motion when you say, "Jesus says" first. If you don't say, "Jesus says" before the command, and they do it anyway, they're out. If they follow a motion that doesn't match the "Jesus says" verbal command, they're out.

The winner is the last one in the game. They become the leader for the next round.

Remind students that God wants us to listen to Jesus and do what He says.

Game: Sword Drill – Remind students that if we want to listen to what Jesus says, we have to know what He said, and we can only know what He said if we read and learn the Bible.

Give each student a Bible. Then, call out the name of one of the books of the Bible. The student who finds that book first wins. To make it a little more difficult, you can call out the chapter and verse of a book or the name of a Biblical person or event.

Remind students how important it is to read and study the Bible on their own so that they can know it well.

Game: Fast Reflexes – Lay out a deck of game cards on a table, face up. The cards could be regular playing cards, UNO cards, Go Fish! cards, etc.

Students gather around the table. You'll call out a type of card (a number, color, shape, etc.). The last student to reach out and touch that type of card is out.

The last student in the game wins and becomes the caller for the next round.

Remind students that we can't wait to follow Jesus. We can't make excuses. We have to obey Him immediately, just like they need to be quick to play this game.

Closing Prayer: Father God, we thank You for sending Your Son, Jesus, to teach us. Help us to listen to and obey Him as You want us to. In Jesus' name we pray, amen.

Recommended Extras

The Transfiguration – free coloring and activity pages

https://freesundayschoolcurriculum.weebly.com/uploads/1/2/5/0/12503916/lesson_57_the_transfiguration.pdf

On the Mountaintop with Jesus – free object lesson, along with free coloring and activity pages

https://www.sermons4kids.com/on_the_mountain_top_with_jesus.htm

Remembering to Give Thanks – Jesus Heals Ten Men with Leprosy

Use this children's Sunday School lesson to show kids the importance of thanking God and how to do that.

Needed: Bibles, a ball

Intro Game: Thanks Toss – Students stand in a circle and randomly toss a ball back and forth. Whenever someone catches the ball, they have to name one thing they're thankful for, but it can't be anything anyone else has said.

Lesson: Ask students, Who is someone that you like to do things with? (Mom, Dad, friend, grandma, grandpa, big brother or sister, etc.)

Now, I want you to think of a time that you were sick and didn't feel good.

(Read Luke 17:11-19 or summarize it with the following story.)

Summary Story: A long time ago, when Jesus was a man on earth, 10 men caught a disease. They were very sick. The disease made ugly, hurtful spots on their skin, and they couldn't be around anyone. They couldn't be with their mom or dad or brother or sister or grandma or grandpa or their friends because if they got close to people, those people might catch the disease too.

The disease was called leprosy. And the people who had it had to live out in the desert by themselves, and they were very sad because they didn't feel good and couldn't be around anyone.

But one day, Jesus met 10 men out in the desert who had leprosy. And He healed them! He told them to simply go to the church and show themselves to the priests, and they would be all better. And that's what happened. As the 10 men started walking to the church, their disease suddenly vanished. The leprosy went away, and they were all better.

Now, I want you to think; If you were one of those ten men and you had been sick and not able to see your family for a long time, what is the first thing you would do when you saw that you were better?

All of the men went off. We're not sure where they went. Maybe they went to see their families. Maybe they went to do something else.

All of the men except one.

One man came running back to Jesus and fell down, kneeling at Jesus' feet, and thanked Jesus.

Jesus was proud of that man because the man thanked Him. But Jesus was sad that the other men didn't come back to thank Him.

Review Questions
What was the good thing that one of the sick men did in the story? (He came back and thanked Jesus for making him better.)

Do you think Jesus likes it when we thank Him for things? (Yes.)

What are some things that you can thank Jesus for? (Giving you your family, dying on the cross for you, loving you, etc.)

What are some ways that we can thank Jesus for the good things He does for us? (Thank Him in prayer, give an offering, sing Him a worship song, do something good that He wants you to do, do something nice for someone else as a way of thanking Jesus, etc.)

So, when something good happens to you, always remember to thank God and Jesus for that good thing, and that make will Jesus happy.

Game: Ten Leper Relay – Divide students into two or more teams. Have one student from each team stand at the opposite end of the play area as the others. That student is "Jesus" for their team.

When you say, "Go!" the first player from each team will run toward their "Jesus" at the opposite end. "Jesus" tags them, and then that player runs back to their team.

The second player then runs toward "Jesus" and does the same. Play continues until the last player reaches "Jesus" and return to their team's starting position. At that point, the last player then returns to "Jesus," and "Jesus" and that player run to the rest of the team together.

The first team to have all of their team members, including "Jesus," reach their starting area wins.

Activity: Acting It Out – Divide students into groups of two or three. Have each group decide on and act out a scene depicting how they can give thanks to God.

Closing Prayer: Jesus, thank You for everything You've done for us and everything You do for us. Help us always to remember to thank You. Amen.

Recommended Extras

One Man Thanks Jesus – free coloring and activity pages

> https://freesundayschoolcurriculum.weebly.com/uploads/1/2/5/0/12503916/lesson_55_one_man_thanks_jesus.pdf

The Thankful Leper – free object lesson, along with free coloring and activity pages

https://www.sermons4kids.com/thankful_leper.htm

Made in the USA
Coppell, TX
16 November 2023

24332340R10042